# HEROIC JOBS

# RESCUE AT SEA

ude

**www.raintreepublishers.co.uk**
Visit our website to find out more information about Raintree books.

**To order:**
☎ Phone 0845 6044371
🖷 Fax +44 (0) 1865 312263
🖳 Email myorders@raintreepublishers.co.uk

Customers from outside the UK please telephone +44 1865 312262

Raintree is an imprint of **Capstone Global Library Limited**, a company incorporated in England and Wales having its registered office at 7 Pilgrim Street, London, EC4V 6LB – Registered company number: 6695582.

Edited by Dan Nunn, Rebecca Rissman, and Catherine Veitch
Designed by Joanne Malivoire
Picture research by Elizabeth Alexander
Originated by Capstone Global Library
Printed and bound in China by CTPS

ISBN 978 1 406 23211 0 (hardback)
15 14 13 12 11
10 9 8 7 6 5 4 3 2 1

ISBN 978 1 406 23218 9 (paperback)
16 15 14 13 12
10 9 8 7 6 5 4 3 2 1

**British Library Cataloguing in Publication Data**
Oxlade, Chris.
Rescue at sea. – (Heroic jobs)
363.1'2381-dc22
A full catalogue record for this book is available from the British Library.

**Acknowledgements**
We would like to thank the following for permission to reproduce photographs: Alamy pp. 4 (© Tim Woodcock), 6 (© Jack Sullivan), 9 (© Tim Jones), 10 (© Simon Price), 13 (© stephen How), 19 (© WaterFrame), 25 (© Mike Greenslade); Corbis pp. 17 (© Andrew Fox), 18 (© Ton Koene/ZUMA Press), 27 (© Andrew Watson/JAI); Getty Images pp. 5 (Peter Macdiarmid), 8 (Hannah Johnston), 11 (Jeff J Mitchell), 14 (Spencer Platt), 15 (Matt Cardy), 21 (Matt Cardy), 22 (Johnson Liu/AFP), 24 (Ed Taylor); iStockphoto p. 12 (© Eric Gevaert); Shutterstock pp. 7 (© Jerry-Rainey), 29 top (© Warren Chan), 29 bottom (© Ruth Black); U.S. Coast Guard pp. 16 (Petty Officer 3rd Class Erik Swanson), 20 (Petty Officer 3rd Class Jon-Paul Rios), 23 (Petty Officer 1st Class David Mosley), 26 (Petty Officer 3rd Class George Degener).

Cover photograph of a Royal National Lifeboat Institute crew on the water at Porthcawl, Wales reproduced with permission of Corbis (© Andrew Fox).

We would like to thank Olivia Milles for her invaluable help in the preparation of this book.

Some words are shown in bold, **like this**. You can find out what they mean by looking in the glossary.

# Contents

# Emergency!

At sea the wind is howling. The waves are as high as a house. A fishing boat is being tossed up and down. Its engine has broken down, and there is a sick fisherman on board. It's time for rescuers to take to the sea and the air.

# Who needs help?

Ship's **crews**, passengers, sailors, oil-rig workers, divers, surfers, and swimmers all work and play at sea. Sometimes they get lost at sea. Sometimes they get sick or injured. Sometimes their ships and boats break down or sink. Then they need to be rescued.

**Did you know?**
A cruise ship has lifeboats with enough room for everyone on board.

# Meet the rescuers

Rescuers work on lifeboats and on the beach. A small lifeboat has a **crew** of two or three. A large lifeboat has a crew of ten or more. Everyone has their own job to do. The person in charge is called the **skipper**.

Lifeguards are rescuers who work at the beach.

# Air crews

The navy, air force, and coastguard have search-and-rescue helicopters. Pilots fly the helicopters. They are very skilled at flying. During a sea rescue they **hover** the helicopter over a ship, even in fierce winds.

Some crew members either jump, or are lowered into the water by a **winch**. They are called swimmers or **winchmen**.

winch

# Dangers of the job

Rescuers in lifeboats and helicopters face super-strong winds, enormous waves, and sometimes very cold water. Lifeboats and **winchmen** sometimes smash into ships and boats that are rolling about in the big waves.

**Did you know?**
In the world's oceans, strong winds can make waves that are more than 30 metres high. That's as high as a ten-storey building!

# Coastal dangers

lifeguard

Rescuers who work on or near the shore face extra dangers. Strong currents can pull lifeguards and other rescuers along the shore or out to sea. Helicopter **crews** are also at risk when they fly close to cliffs in strong winds.

Coastguards often battle through **surf** to make a rescue.

# Rescue boats

Rescuers use different sorts of rescue boats. Big lifeboats can travel far out to sea in very bad weather. Their powerful engines push them along at high speeds. Small, high-speed lifeboats are used for rescues close to shore.

**Did you know?**
When big lifeboats get knocked over by a wave, some can flip back up the right way. This is called self-righting.

# Rescue equipment

Rescuers carry lots of equipment in their boats and helicopters. They take **first aid** equipment to treat injured or sick people. They take stretchers to carry people to safety. Rescue swimmers carry radios.

Lifeboat **crew** members wear waterproof survival suits in case they fall in the water.

A search-and-rescue helicopter has lots of different equipment.

# To the rescue!

**Seafarers** who get into trouble call for help by radio, or by telephone. They might also let off a bright **flare**, like a firework. It is important to tell the rescue team the following information:

- where they are
- what trouble they are in
- a description of their boat
- how many people are on board.

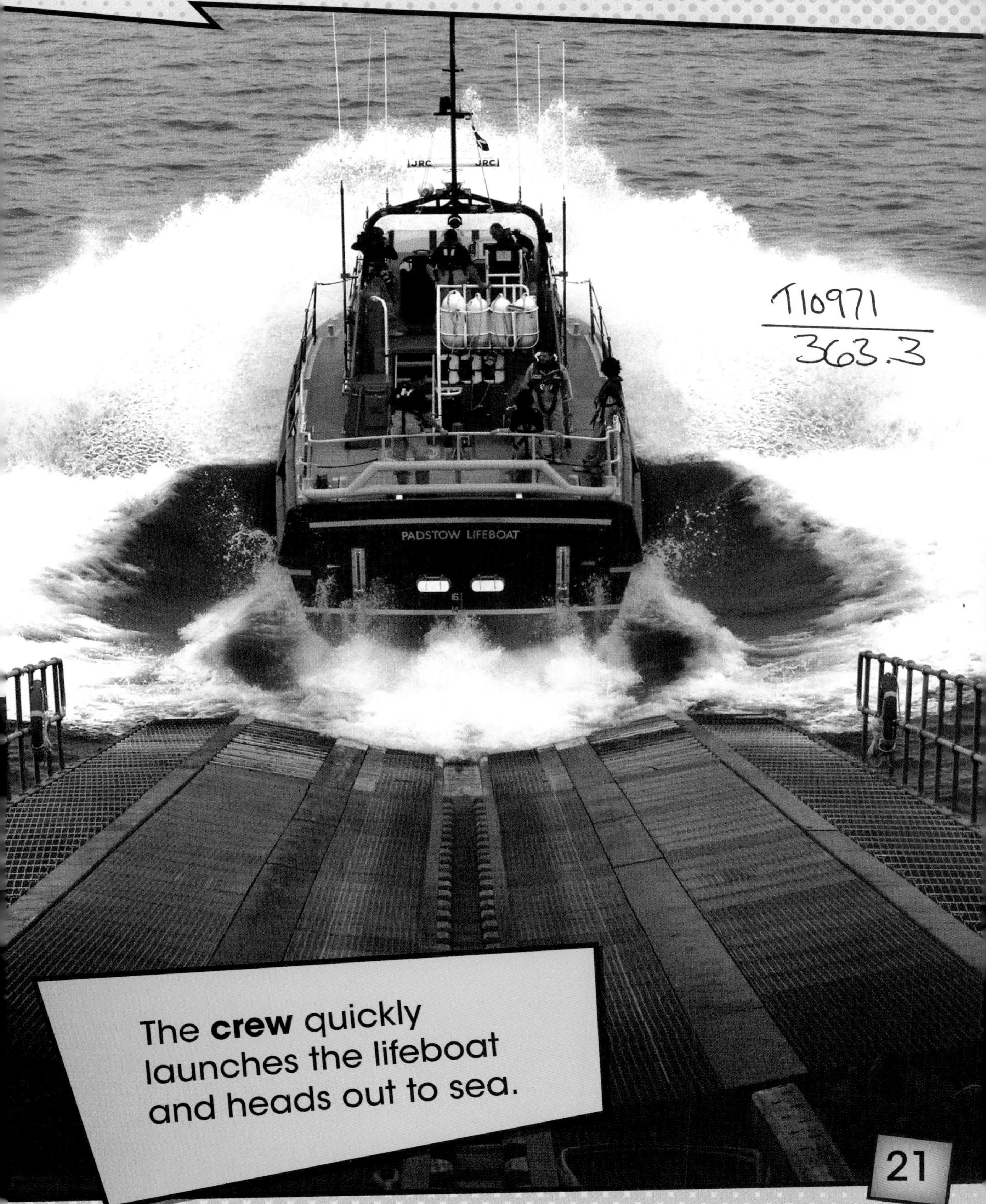




The **crew** quickly launches the lifeboat and heads out to sea.

# Helicopter rescues

A helicopter **crew** is called into action if an emergency happens in a place that a lifeboat can't reach. It helps to search for small boats and people in the sea. Helicopters also take injured or sick people to hospital.

**Did you know?**
Long-range search aircraft look for people who are lost very far out at sea, where helicopters and boats can't go.

# Beach rescue!

Many heroic rescues take place in the sea close to beaches. If somebody gets into trouble, other boaters, surfers, or swimmers raise the alarm. Beach lifeguards rush into the water to help. They pull the person back to the beach, and give **first aid**.

This lifeguard is rushing to the rescue on a jet ski.

# Becoming a rescuer

Rescuers need many different skills. Members of lifeboat **crews** must have experience of going to sea. Beach lifeguards must be strong swimmers and have good **first aid** skills. Helicopter crews need the most training.

These men are training to put out a fire.

In Australia, children can join the junior lifeguards to learn about the job.

# Staying safe at sea

Many emergencies at sea and at the beach can be avoided by following some simple rules:

- Never swim in the sea alone.
- Always take notice of warning signs.
- Be aware of the tide.
- Always wear a **flotation device**, like a life jacket, when boating.
- If there is an emergency, tell a lifeguard, or phone the emergency services. Never go to the rescue yourself.

**Did you know?**
There are different emergency telephone numbers in the world:
- Australia: 000
- most of Europe: 112
- UK: 999
- United States: 911

DANGER
NO SWIMMING

# Glossary

**crew**  group of people who work on a ship or boat

**first aid**  help given to an injured or sick person before they are taken to a hospital

**flare**  item that produces a very bright flame. It is used as a signal for help by people at sea who are in trouble.

**flotation device**  lifejacket or a buoyancy aid that stops you from sinking in the water

**seafarer**  person who travels at sea, such as a yacht sailor or a fisherman

**skipper**  person who is in charge of the crew of a ship or boat

**surf**  line of foam made by waves crashing against the shore

**winch**  machine that winds in or lets out wire. It can be used to lift people in and out of a helicopter.

**winchman**  member of a helicopter rescue crew who lowers down to pick up people from the sea